LOOK WHAT TAILS CAN DO

CAN DO

LOOK What
ANIMALS
Can Do

LOOK WHAT TAILS CAN DO

BY DM SOUZA

Lerner Books · London · New York · Minneapolis

photo on page 2: **The tails of kangaroos help them balance when sitting, hopping or even fighting.**

This book was first published in the United States of America in 2007.

First published in the United Kingdom in 2008 by
Lerner Books,
Dalton House,
60 Windsor Avenue,
London SW19 2RR

Website address: www.lernerbooks.co.uk

This edition was updated and edited for UK publication by Discovery Books Ltd., Unit 3, 37 Watling Street, Leintwardine, Shropshire SY7 0LW

Words in **bold** type are explained in the glossary on page 44.

British Library Cataloguing in Publication Data

Souza, D. M. (Dorothy M.)

  Look what tails can do. - (Look what animals can do)
  1. Tail - Juvenile literature 2. Tail - Adaptation -
  Juvenile literature 3. Animal behavior - Juvenile
  literature
  I. Title
  591.4

  ISBN-13: 978 1 58013 396 8

Printed in China

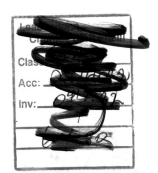

TABLE OF CONTENTS

LOOK AROUND
TAILS ARE EVERYWHERE

Some tails are long and skinny. Others are short and bushy. There are flat tails, curly tails, striped tails and dotted tails. There are scaly tails, prickly tails, feathery tails and hairy tails.

Ring-tailed lemurs hold their long striped tails high when they move around.

No matter what they look like, tails are important body parts for many animals. Think of a monkey trying to move from branch to branch without its tail. How would a fish swim without its tail? How would cows, horses or giraffes swat flies and insects without their tails?

Most of the time, tails help animals keep their balance as they run or climb. But tails do other things too. Let's take a look at a few animals with amazing tails and see how they use them.

Armadillo lizards put their tails in their mouths to protect their soft bellies from enemies.

ALL-PURPOSE TAIL

A grey squirrel uses its tail in many ways. On rainy days the squirrel curls its tail over its head like an umbrella. On cold nights it wraps its tail around itself like a blanket.

During fights the squirrel flicks its tail back and forth to distract its enemy. Sometimes during a fight, it holds its tail up like a shield to soften blows. But when the squirrel is searching for food its tail becomes a lifesaver.

A young girl fills a bird feeder with sunflower seeds. A squirrel watches from a treetop. As soon as the girl leaves, the squirrel races down the tree.

The squirrel sits high in a tree getting ready to make its move.

Halfway down, the squirrel leaps into the air. It swings its tail from side to side, steering towards the feeder. Thump! Its tail helps the squirrel make a perfect landing.

The squirrel jumps onto a clothes line with a mouthful of seeds. It races across the wire with its tail swinging from side to side. It uses its tail for balance the way an acrobat uses outstretched arms. When the squirrel reaches a post, it leaps back onto the tree. It makes another perfect landing. Where would the grey squirrel be without its tail?

The squirrel's tail is perfect for helping it keep its balance.

BUSY TAIL

A beaver swims across a moonlit pond. It has a small branch in its mouth. Nearby another beaver paddles along. It is pulling a branch through the water.

The beavers are busy every night. Before winter they must store food for themselves and their **kits**. They must repair their **lodge** and add more sticks, grass and mud to it. They will also build a dam to raise the water level in the pond. Then their food supply will not freeze in the deep water.

Beavers are strong swimmers because of their paddle-shaped tails.

The beavers' tails help in many ways. They are flat, wide and covered with scales, like those of a fish. When beavers swim forwards, their tails move up and down. When they want to change directions, they swing their tails to one side or the other.

While a beaver is standing on land cutting a tree, its wide tail serves as a stool. When the beaver is walking on its hind legs, the tail keeps it balanced.

If a **predator** suddenly appears, the tail sounds an alarm. One beaver slaps its tail against the water with a mighty splash. The sound is as loud as a pistol shot. All the beavers in the area know it's time to swim to safety. Yes, the beaver's tail does many things on land and in the water.

Beavers don't just use their tails for swimming. Their tails are very useful on land too.

ONE OF A KIND

This skinny tail is long and hairless. You might think it belongs to a rat. But it can do something the rat's tail cannot. It can grab objects. The tail belongs to an opossum. It's called a **prehensile** tail.

When an opossum is climbing a tree, its tail acts like an extra paw. The tail grabs one branch until the opossum's paws can grab onto another. If the animal is collecting fruit, the tail curls around a branch. The opossum can then reach for fruit with both of its front paws.

Opossums' tails wrap tightly around tree limbs. Their tails' grip gives them extra support while climbing.

The opossum's tail also plays a role during nest building. The female rakes together leaves and grass for her nest. Then she grabs the pile with her tail and carries it away.

Young opossums often ride on their mother's back. They hold on by curling their tails around her fur. If they don't weigh too much, the young can also hang from branches by their tails. It must be fun having a prehensile tail.

Young opossums travel on their mother's back and hold on with their tails.

POISONOUS TAIL

Darkness covers the desert. A yellowish-brown scorpion crawls out from under a log. It has been hiding from the hot rays of the sun. Now in the cool of evening it is ready for a meal.

The scorpion stands on its eight legs. It cannot see very well, but it can feel movements. It raises two large **pincers** near the front of its body. Its long tail armed with a stinger curves over its back.

A cockroach zigzags across the sand. It does not see the scorpion. It comes close to where the creature is standing.

The dark stinger at the end of the scorpion's tail holds deadly poison.

In a second the large pincers reach out and grab hold of the insect. The cockroach struggles but cannot escape. Quickly the scorpion's tail strikes. It fills the insect's body with deadly poison.

In minutes the cockroach is lifeless. Slowly the scorpion tears it apart. After it has finished its meal it rests.

Scorpions may wait for weeks or even months between meals. They do not need much food. But when they do get hungry their poison-filled tails are always ready to strike.

Scorpions capture and kill insects with their large pincers and deadly tails.

TALKING TAILS

If you have a pet dog, you probably know that its tail often sends messages. A wagging tail lets you know that your dog is glad to see you. A drooping tail gives you a clue that your dog is not feeling well. A tail between its legs may signal that the dog is frightened.

Wolves are related to dogs and live together in **packs** or groups. They travel and hunt together. Members of the pack communicate with their tails.

Wolves are social animals. They live most of their lives with other wolves.

Wolves warn one another of danger by pointing their tails straight out. Pups let others know they want to play by wagging their tails.

The **alpha**, or head wolf, shows it is top wolf by holding its tail high. The **omega** shows it is the lowest-ranking wolf by lowering its tail. Like a pet dog's tail, wolves' tails say many things without ever making a sound.

You can tell by how they hold their tails that one wolf is weaker than the other.

A WRIGGLING TAIL

A skink, a lizard with shiny skin, warms itself in the morning sun. It flicks out its tongue, trying to pick up the scent of food. An insect, earthworm or spider would make a tasty meal.

Suddenly a cricket lands nearby. The skink jerks forwards. But the cricket is too quick. It hops away and disappears deeper into the forest.

A cat has been watching the action. It crouches low and creeps closer. The skink flicks out its tongue again, but it's too late. Slam! One of the cat's paws comes down on top of the skink's shiny blue tail.

This skink has five light-coloured stripes on its body. They run from the lizard's neck to the tip of its tail.

The cat looks at its catch. The bright blue tail is wriggling wildly on the ground. But there is no skink. The animal has escaped.

Many lizards escape predators by leaving their tails behind. Their tails can break off in several places without harming the animals. In a short time a new tail grows back. But until it does the lizard must be careful. If it gets caught again it has no wriggling tail to leave behind.

Skinks' tails break off so they can escape a predator.

33

A DANGEROUS TAIL

Did you know that porcupines have hidden weapons in their tails? These weapons are called **quills**. They are stiff, hollow hairs that are very sharp and pointed like needles.

Quills are hidden in the animal's fur. More than 30,000 are on the porcupine's head, back and tail. Most of the time the quills lie flat. But if the animal is frightened, its quills and long hairs stand up. They make the porcupine look like a giant pincushion.

Porcupines have sharp quills on their heads, backs and tails. Their quills usually lie flat.

If a porcupine meets a predator, the porcupine clicks its teeth together. If the predator does not leave, the porcupine puts its nose between its feet. Next it turns its back end towards the enemy. Swat! The tail strikes and several quills may get stuck in the animal's face.

Once a quill enters the skin it is hard to remove. Quills that land in animals' eyes can blind them. Quills in their mouths can make it hard for them to eat. Most animals try to stay away from the porcupine's dangerous tail.

Porcupines stick their quills straight out when they feel threatened.

MORE TAILS

Wolves and dogs are not the only animals with tails that send messages. White-tailed deer have short tan or brown tails. When danger is near, one deer will flip its tail up. White fur underneath flashes and sends a warning to others, 'Run for your life'.

White-tailed deer show the white fur underneath their tails to warn that danger is near.

A rattlesnake's buzzing tail tells predators, 'Stay away'. A skunk's tail raised over its head says, 'Leave if you don't want to get sprayed'.

Male peacocks and turkeys use their tails to win mates. They spread their feathers like fans. Then they **strut** around waiting for females to notice them.

Male peacocks use their huge colourful tails to impress females.

Some animals use their tails to catch meals. Alligators often wait along river banks for creatures they can eat. When a meal arrives, the gators swing their powerful tails. One blow can throw an animal into the water. There the gator easily makes a catch.

Alligators use their strong tails for swimming and catching meals.

Manatees have large paddle-shaped [tails. These] move up and down when the giants [swim]. But when they are resting the heavy [tails act like] anchors. They keep the manatees ne[ar the bottom of] the water.

Manatees' tails keep them at the seabed so they can rest.

Ring-tailed lemurs sometimes fight with their tails. They have 'stink fights' with one another. Each lemur rubs its long tail across scent spots on its body. Then it spreads the smell by waving its tail over the head of the other lemur. The lemur with a 'stink' that lasts the longest wins the fight.

A ring-tailed lemur stands up with its long tail flying high.

Birds from Central America called quetzals have long tail feathers. The male's feathers are almost three times as long as its body. The quetzal flies high and then swoops down. Its brilliant tail floats across the sky like a colourful scarf. Now that's a tail to top all tails.

Quetzals' colourful tail feathers flow behind them while they fly.

GLOSSARY

alpha: the top wolf, or leader, in a pack

kits: the young of beavers

lodge: home of a family of beavers

omega: the lowest-ranking wolf in a pack

packs: groups of animals such as wolves

pincers: a pair of claws used for grabbing

predator: an animal that hunts other animals for food

prehensile: able to curl around or grab onto objects

quills: stiff, pointed, hollow hairs on the tail, head and back of a porcupine

strut: to walk proudly

FURTHER READING

BOOKS

Butz, Christopher. *Lemurs* (Animals of the Rain Forest) Raintree, 2002.

Miles, Elizabeth. *Tails* (Why Do Animal Have) Heinemann, 2003.

Pipe, Jim. *Paws, Tails and Whiskers* Franklin Watts Ltd, 2004.

Schaefer, Lola M. *Squirrels* (My Big Backyard) Heinemann, 2004.

Solway, Andrew. *Deadly Spiders and Scorpions* (Wild Predators) Heinemann, 2005.

Turner, Matt. *Beavers* (Secret World of...) Raintree, 2003.

Whitehouse, Patricia. *Opossums* (What's Awake?) Heinemann, 2003.

WEBSITES

About Porcupines
    http://www.nativetech.org/quill/porcupin.html
    If you've ever wondered what a porcupine quill looks like, this
    Native American site shows a close-up of one. It also has fun
    facts about porcupines.

The Beaver
    http://www.saskschools.ca/~gregory/animals/bvr.html
    This Canadian school site is filled with photos and facts about
    beavers and their amazing tails.

Squirrels
    www.squirrel.info
    This website is dedicated to the conservation of squirrels in
    the United Kingdom.

Taronga Zoo
    http://www.zoo.nsw.gov.au/index.htm
    This Australian website is packed with information and
    pictures about a wide variety of different animals.

INDEX

Page numbers in *italics* refer to illustrations.

PHOTO ACKNOWLEDGEMENTS

Images reproduced with permission from:
© Martin Harvey/Peter Arnold, Inc., p 2; © Nigel J Dennis/Photo Researchers, Inc., p 6; © Rod Patterson; Gallo Images/CORBIS, p 9; © Gary W Carter/ CORBIS, p 11; © J. Paling/OSF/Animals Animals, p 13; © Erwin & Peggy Bauer/Animals Animals, p 14; © Lynda Richardson/Peter Arnold, Inc., p 17; © Steve Maslowski/Visuals Unlimited, p 19; © Phyllis Greenberg/Animals Animals, p 20; © Roger De La Harpe/Animals Animals, p 23; © Charles Melton/Visuals Unlimited, p 24; © Art Wolfe, p 26; © Tom & Pat Leeson/Photo Researchers, Inc., p 29; © Scott W Smith/Animals Animals, p 31; © W Cheng/OSF/Animals Animals, p 33; © Tim Davis/Photo Researchers, Inc., p 34; © Joe McDonald/Animals Animals, p 37; © Stephen J Krasemann/Photo Researchers, Inc., p 38; © Dr William Weber/Visuals Unlimited, p 39; © George McCarthy/CORBIS, p 40; © Brandon Cole/Visuals Unlimited, p 41; © Frank Krahmer/zefa/CORBIS, p 42; © Gregory G Dimijian, M D/Photo Researchers, Inc., p 43.

Front cover: © Steve Maslowski/Photo Researchers, Inc.